Growing up!

Taddy the Toad

by Jane Burton

SIMON & SCHUSTER

LONDON • SYDNEY • NEW YORK • TOKYO • SINGAPORE • TORONTO

First published in Great Britain in 1990 by Simon & Schuster Young Books

Simon & Schuster Young Books   Simon Schuster Ltd
Wolsey House, Wolsey Road, Hemel Hempstead, Herts HP2 4SS

Conceived, designed and produced by
Belitha Press Ltd
31 Newington Green, London N16 9PU

Printed and bound in Hong Kong
for Imago Press

ISBN 0 7500 0427 4

First published 1989 in the United States
by Random House Inc, New York, and
simultaneously in Canada by Random
House of Canada Limited, Toronto,
under the title *Happy the Toad*

Toads are spawning in the big pond. The male rides piggyback on the female, his arms round her tummy. She lays her eggs in jelly strings – called 'spawn' – as she swims along.

Each little round black blob in the spawn is an egg. Soon it starts to grow a head and a tail. In a few days it begins to wriggle and uncurl. The first little tadpole wriggles until she swims out of the jelly.

One week old

Now Taddy has a long tail for swimming and a bunch of feathery gills on each side of her head for breathing. She swims away from the old jelly and sucks onto a duckweed stem.

Three weeks old

The tadpoles are feeding among blanket weed which gives off bubbles in the sun. The bubbles lift the weed out of the water and Taddy is nearly stranded. She struggles to swim out of the weed.

Four weeks old

Skin has grown over Taddy's gills. She can swim really fast by flailing her tail. All the tadpoles swim at the surface in a wriggling black shoal.

Eight weeks old

The tadpoles have grown hind legs. Front legs are growing too, making a bulge on each side of their heads. When the front legs are ready, they will suddenly pop out of the breathing hole in the gill covers. Soon the tadpoles will start to breathe air.

Twelve weeks old

No longer a tadpole, Taddy is nearly a toadlet. She has stopped eating and is living off her tail. As her body grows, her tail shrinks. She is getting ready to leave the water.

Sixteen weeks old

One damp day after a thunderstorm, all the toadlets climb out of the pond and crawl away to begin their life on land.

Taddy battles through a 'forest' of moss stems. They are really not very tall, but she is *very* tiny.

Five months old

Each night during the summer, Taddy crawls about over the heather looking for tiny insects to snap up. She is growing fast all the time. Gradually she travels right away from the pond.

Six months old

Taddy reaches the woods where Warty, a grown-up toad, lives. Warty watches Taddy as if he might eat her. Taddy stays quite still. Warty needs to see his prey move before deciding to snap it up. Taddy doesn't move, so Warty loses interest and crawls on.

It has been raining, but now it has stopped.
Toads like to be out exploring when it is cool and
damp. So do snails.

Nannus the snail has been eating a toadstool,
rasping it with its toothy tongue. Now it starts to
glide away, weaving its eye-stalks. Taddy notices
the movement of an eye-stalk and gets ready to
snap at it. It could be something to eat.

Nannus seems not to notice Taddy, and just
glides towards her. Taddy puts up a foot and
shoves the snail in the face. Nannus quickly
draws in its eye-stalks to protect its delicate eyes.

Taddy starts to creep past while Nannus can't
see, but the snail zooms its eyes out again and
comes down by mistake – right on top of Taddy!
Snails only eat vegetables, so Nannus means no
harm. Taddy slips out from underneath, just a
little slimy.

Eight months old

Taddy is a 'cold-blooded' animal – her body is always the same temperature as the world around her. In the summer she is lively, but now that the nights are cold, Taddy is too cold to feed. The colder she is, the slower she moves, and her skin turns black with cold.

Before she gets so cold that she cannot move at all, Taddy finds a frostproof place in which to 'hibernate' or pass the winter. She digs into a hole beneath a log. Snails are already clustering there, cementing themselves into their shells.

Taddy and the snails go into hibernation. They are not exactly asleep but they are so cold they are 'torpid' – not moving, not eating, hardly breathing. They stay like this all through the cold winter weather.

In the spring, the sun warms the ground again. Taddy and the snails gradually warm up enough to come creeping out of hibernation.

Eighteen months old

All through her second summer Taddy is hardly seen at all. She leads a secret life because of her need to keep cool and damp all the time. So she hides during the day in a damp place under a log, and only comes out at night, when it is always cool and damp.

At the end of the summer a storm blows all the leaves off the nut trees early. It rains and rains until the ground is waterlogged. A toad must have dampness, but it hates a flood!

Taddy is washed out of her home and has to swim. She clambers out of the water onto a little island. Perched on the edge she looks out across a vast puddle. Suddenly the 'island' rocks slightly, then it starts to turn.

The 'island' turns round! A sharp nose pokes out of it, and an eye appears. A head rises from the water. Taddy backs away. The terrapin untucks its feet and paddles across the puddle, carrying Taddy to the far side.

Two years old

Warm days in spring wake Taddy out of her second hibernation. In a damp spot among primroses she makes her home in a flowerpot.

Emma meets her early one evening, and bounces round her, wanting to play. She picks Taddy up, but the toad oozes poison from her skin and Emma spits her out at once. Taddy crawls home unhurt, but Emma froths at the mouth and shakes her head, trying to get rid of the foul taste of toad.

One day Taddy feels dry and thirsty. She starts across the lawn, heading for the garden pond.

Oops! Taddy almost steps on a grass snake basking in the sun. Grass snakes eat toads! Taddy is very alarmed. She stands on tiptoe and puffs herself up with air. But the snake is only a small one, and Taddy looks enormous, all puffed up. The snake is just as frightened of Taddy and slithers hastily away.

In the pond Taddy has a long drink, but not through her mouth. She sits on a lily pad and absorbs the water through her skin.

All through her third summer Taddy eats and grows. She snaps up whatever small moving creatures she comes across in the night. When she meets a beetle grub tramping along, she watches it to be sure it is good toad food. Also she has to judge where to aim her tongue. She concentrates, motionless.

Suddenly, *plop!* Taddy's pink tongue shoots out. The grub is caught on the sticky tip and flipped into her mouth, all in a split second.

By autumn Taddy is fully grown. For the third time she goes into hibernation.

Three years old

Taddy is out of hibernation and on the move again. She starts to crawl towards the big pond where she was born. Now that she is grown up, she is ready to spawn. Other adult toads are crawling towards the pond from all around.

Taddy has a long, long way to crawl, but
nothing can stop her. She climbs walls, hops out
of ditches, clambers over the heather. She even
has to cross a busy road. Cars hurtle by, their
headlights dazzling her. Many toads are
squashed but Taddy crosses safely. She reaches
the pond at last and splashes in.

    Taddy's arrival in the pond makes a big
commotion. The males have been waiting for
females to arrive. Bufo grabs Taddy and they
swim about together underwater. Taddy lays her
spawn while Bufo sheds his sperm over it to
fertilize the eggs.

After Taddy has finished spawning, Bufo lets
go of her. She rests a while, then leaves the pond.
She takes no care of her eggs or tadpoles. Slowly
she makes her way back to her flowerpot home for
the summer.